THE Tao OF STAR WARS

D0033975

THE Tao OF STAR WARS

BY JOHN M. PORTER, M.D.

JOHN M. PORTER

VI

INTRODUCTION

The *Tao Te Ching*, after the Bible, is the most translated book in the world. It is nearly 2600 years old and along with Confucianism forms the philosophical basis of almost the entire Chinese culture. It is the basic text of Taoism. Taoist roots touch on almost every aspect of life from how to arrange furniture in your house (*feng shui*) and medicine (*qi gong*) to guidance for the future (*I Ching*). Despite this widespread influence it is a book of only 81 chapters and slightly more than 5000 characters. Its reputed author, Lao Tzu, was an old wise man born in either 604 or 571 BCE. Faced with a corrupt, competitive, egocentric society, which had lost its way (sound familiar?), he left society riding upon an ox. He felt that society had lost the Tao and that was the cause of the decline of the civilization.

> *When the great Tao is forgotten,*
> *Goodness and piety appear.*
> *When the body's intelligence declines,*
> *Cleverness and knowledge step forth.*
> *When there is no peace in the family,*
> *Filial piety begins.*
> *When the country falls into chaos,*
> *Patriotism is born.*
>
> **—Chapter 18**

At the request of the border guard at the mountain pass, Lao Tzu wrote the *Tao Te Ching*. He then went into the mountains and was never seen again. Scholars debate as to whether or not Lao Tzu was the sole author or if the text was the compilation of an extensive oral tradition. That point may be of scholarly interest but is not of practical interest because followers have become "Taoists" not "Lao Tzuists."

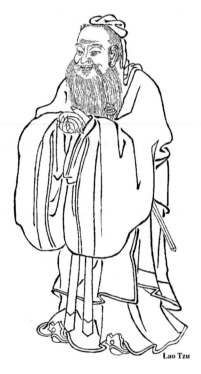

Lao Tzu

In the past several decades there has been a rekindled interest in the Tao. The reasons for this are varied. Humans have always had an insatiable hunger for spiritual guidance, which quite frankly, has not recently been fulfilled by traditional organized religion. We have sought out many things to fill this spiritual void from Pentecostal Christianity, Science and Technology, and New Age philosophies, to Eastern religions and philosophies. In this search, Westerners have "rediscovered" Taoism.

This search is also responsible, in part, for the popularity of the Star Wars series. As Star Wars creator George Lucas states in the *USA Today*, "There are mythical underpinnings to the movie and archetypes that have been around for thousands and thousands of years, most of them before Christianity." This has led to people actually turning to Star Wars to fill this spiritual void. Moreover, it is inspiring people to explore other spiritual options, including Taoism. This is the inspiration for this book: How does the Star Wars series lead to an understanding of Taoism as a viable spiritual option in today's world?

QUOTES FROM THE TAO TE CHING: Unless otherwise noted, they are taken from Stephen Mitchell's translation of the *Tao Te Ching*, New York: HarperCollins Publishers, 1988.

HOW TO READ THIS BOOK: It can be read straight through in one sitting. You can also read the overview of Taoism to get its general flavor and then to pick different chapters that will elaborate on the overview, using Star Wars analogies. Of course, as in life, the choice is yours. I hope that you enjoy reading this book half as much as I have enjoyed writing it.

X

TABLE OF CONTENTS

does not have to be the case. We shall be speaking only of the philosophical aspects of Taoism. The basis of the philosophy is contained in the *Tao Te Ching*, presumably written by Lao Tzu, as discussed in the Introduction. The book's 81 chapters are divided into two parts, intermingled and intimately related. They are the Tao and Te. Ching means the classic text. Thus it is the classic text of the Tao and Te.

The Chinese character for **TAO** is composed of two separate characters.

On the left, it means, "to run," while on the right it is a face. Thus, Tao is a person running along a path. Following the Tao means following a living path. Other interpretations of the word are the way, the way the universe works, and the way to live in harmony with the way things are. It has even been translated in a similar fashion to the Greek word "logos." It is all encompassing as well as an active process.

TE is even more difficult to define. It has been defined as virtue, power, integrity, and innate moral rectitude. The Tao expresses itself through Te, being the vehicle used to move one in the Tao, to drive along the path, so to speak. Te is not pursued but exists innately in a person. It is not defined by a man-made moral code, nor is it an ethical idea to be debated but is the essential nature of the universe and therefore is in all beings.

The basic Taoist viewpoint is that the individual should seek the truth by means of a patient, accepting focus on natural patterns and influences. In this there are several basic tenets and qualities that one who follows the Tao may exhibit. These include:

EMPTINESS: The Tao is all that exists, but at the same time it is the nothingness from which everything comes. Emptiness, void, non-being, or nothingness is sometimes a difficult concept to grasp. We can hold onto the tangible but not the intangible.

> *There was something formless and perfect*
> *Before the universe was born.*
> *It is serene. Empty.*
> *Solitary. Unchanging.*
> *Infinite. Eternally present.*
> *It is the mother of the universe.*
> *For lack of a better name,*
> *I call it Tao.*
>
> **—Chapter 25**

This is similar to the creation in the *Book of Genesis* in which "the earth was without form, and void." It is from nothingness that creation springs. Also related to the concept of emptiness is usefulness. This is a seeming paradox. How can emptiness or void be useful?

We join spokes together in a wheel,
But it is the center hole
That makes the wagon move.

We shape clay into a pot,
But it is the emptiness inside
That holds whatever we want.

We hammer wood for a house,
But it is the inner space
That makes it livable.

We work with being,
But non-being is what we use.

—Chapter 11

The utility of emptiness also applies to the mind. The beginner's mind is an empty mind, not full of preconceived notions and prejudices and thus ready to experience the world.

ACCEPTANCE: Acceptance is at the very essence of the Tao. It is one of the most misunderstood precepts of Taoism. It does not mean fatalism or helplessness. It means acting within the framework of the circumstances. It is a dynamic action. One should simply ascertain what the situation requires and then implement what one feels is best. One has to accept things as they are and the first order of acceptance is to accept oneself, completely. This is followed by accepting the details in one's life.

> *The master sees things as they are,*
> *Without trying to control them.*
> *She lets them go their own way,*
> *And resides at the center of the circle.*
> **—Chapter 29**

> *Accept the world as it is*
> *If you accept the world,*
> *The Tao will be luminous inside you*
> *And you will return to your primal self.*
> **—Chapter 28**

Acceptance is so all-encompassing that it includes the principles flexibility, detachment, patience, *wu wei*, and present moment living.

PATIENCE: Patience is one of the three treasures of Taoism, along with simplicity and compassion.

> *I have just three things to teach:*
> *Simplicity, patience, compassion.*
> *These three are your greatest treasures.*
> *...Patient with both friends and enemies,*
> *you accord with the way things are.*
>
> **—Chapter 67**

As with acceptance, which is intimately related to patience, one must first be patient with oneself and then with the details of one's life.

> *Do you have the patience to wait*
> *Till your mud settles and the water is clear?*
> *Can you remain unmoving*
> *Till the right action arises by itself.*
>
> **—Chapter 15**

Equanimity describes this concept well. It encompasses remaining calm and centered, especially under stress. As such, it then becomes a source of action.

COMPASSION: This is the second of the three great treasures of Taoism.

> *I have just three things to teach:*
> *Simplicity, patience, compassion.*
> *These three are your greatest treasures.*
> *...compassionate toward yourself,*
> *you reconcile all beings in the world.*
> **—Chapter 67**

Put simply, compassion is love, the love for all beings. This stems from the Taoist principle of unity, in which all of the world is connected with and flows in the Tao. Love flows from this naturally. Compassion is the innate expression of our goodness, an expression of Te.

SIMPLICITY: This is the third of the three great treasures of Taoism.

> *I have just three things to teach:*
> *Simplicity, patience, compassion.*
> *These three are your greatest treasures.*
> *...Simple in actions and in thoughts,*
> *you return to the source of being.*
>
> **—Chapter 67**

By discarding arrogance, complexity, and numerous other things that get in the way you will discover the secret that life is fun. You have the ability to enjoy the simple and the quiet, the natural and the plain. Along with that comes the ability to do things spontaneously and have them work. Be what you are, not what you have been taught you should be.

> *When you are content to be simply yourself*
> *And don't compare or compete,*
> *Everybody will respect you.*
>
> **—Chapter 8**

P'U- THE UNCARVED BLOCK: It is the concept of the simple, uncluttered natural man and his way of life. As with the other basic tenets or qualities, the principle of the uncarved block is related to other principles, specifically simplicity and Te. *P'u* means that things in their original nature and simplicity contain their own natural power. This power can be easily spoiled or even lost when that inner simplicity is changed. This strength also comes from being in harmony with the Tao.

He who is in harmony with the Tao
Is like a newborn child.
Its bones are soft, its muscles are weak,
But its grip is powerful.
It doesn't know about the union
Of male and female,
Yet its penis can stand erect,
So intense is its vital power.
It can scream its head off all day,
Yet it never becomes hoarse,
So complete is its harmony.

—**Chapter 55**

WU WEI: This may be the most misunderstood of all the precepts of Taoism. "Nonaction or inaction" are perhaps the best direct translations of *wu wei*.

> *Act without doing;*
> *Work without effort.*
>
> **—Chapter 63**

Nonaction or inaction is almost a heretical thought in western society. However, true *wu wei* is the most efficient possible action, the most spontaneous possible action and often the most creative action. It is not the life of a sloth or laziness, but one in which the least possible effort yields the most effective and productive outcome. Actions come from a more intuitive, spontaneous, and creative area of the mind. The closest analogy would be when an athlete is "in the zone." The actions are not coming from the thinking or calculating area of the mind. Obviously, this is not the same as doing nothing.

> *The master does nothing,*
> *Yet he leaves nothing undone.*
> *The ordinary man is always doing things,*
> *Yet many things are left to be done.*

The kind man does something,
Yet something remains undone.
The just man does something,
And leaves many things to be done.
The moral man does something,
And when no one responds
He rolls up his sleeves and uses force.
—Chapter 38

Intimately related to *wu wei* is harmony, specifically being in harmony with Tao. The Tao functions with effortless ease and so does the person in harmony with it.

The Tao never does anything,
Yet through it all things are done.
—Chapter 37

HUMILITY: In humility exists one of the many paradoxes in Taoism. It is in humility that greatness arises.

> *All streams flow to the sea*
> *Because it is lower than they are.*
> *Humility gives it its power.*
>
> **—Chapter 66**

In the pursuit of the glittering prizes of fame, wealth, and power we become entrapped in an artificial world of intrigue, ego, and false values. This cuts us off from our essential nature.

> *The master never reaches for the great;*
> *Thus she achieves greatness*
>
> **—Chapter 63**

Closely related to humility is the concept of yielding. In fact,

> *Yielding is the way of the Tao.*
>
> **—Chapter 40**

Both humility and yielding are exemplified by water. There is power in yielding, however, it is not the power of effort. As the renowned martial artist Bruce Lee said, "Be like water my friend."

> *Nothing in the world*
> *Is as soft and yielding as water.*
> *Yet for dissolving the hard and inflexible,*
> *Nothing can surpass it.*
> **—Chapter 78**

Another related concept (since the Tao involves oneness and unity, of course, all the concepts are related) is noncontention. If you don't contend, no one can contend with you. By not displaying yourself, you appear bright. By not insisting that you are right, the truth can become manifest. By not boasting of achievements, achievements are noticed.

> *Because she competes with no one,*
> *No one can compete with her.*
> **—Chapter 66**

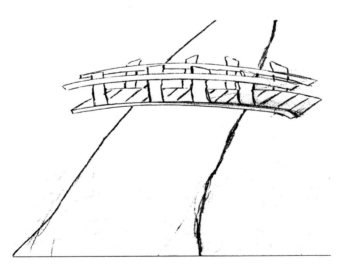

LIFE EXPERIENCE: Knowledge and experience do not always speak the same language. Knowledge that comes from experience is more valuable than knowledge that does not. The only true way to understand the Tao is to directly experience it. To understand you must experience. To experience you must practice, i.e., live. All teachings are mere references. The truest experience is living your own life. The essence of this is found in the Chinese character *lian*, which means to practice or to experience. When the students went to the ancients to learn Tao, the masters emphasized lian. As long as the student practiced, then understanding of Tao was possible.

PRESENT MOMENT LIVING: As with all of the other tenets or qualities, living in the present moment is linked to other concepts, but especially to the value of experience discussed above. The key is to live each moment to the fullest.

> *The master gives himself up*
> *To whatever the moment brings.*
>
> **—Chapter 50**

Tao is a path, as is life. In fact, life from birth to death has Tao as the connecting line. Experience the moment from A to B, not A to Z. The journey is the key, not the destination. Enjoying that is the key to life. Logically, the space between the rewards is longer than the time of the rewards themselves. Remember that the Olympic champion trains for years, for what, at most minutes of glory.

The Present

You cannot see it coming,
  It is always there.

You cannot see it leaving,
  It is always there.

The present...experience it.

CHAPTER TWO

THE FORCE AS THE TAO

In terms of definition, the Force is almost as nebulous as the Tao. It is that way on purpose. George Lucas stated: "I read a lot of books about mythology and theories behind mythology; one of the books was *The Hero with a Thousand Faces* by Joseph Campbell, but there were many others, maybe as many as fifty books. I basically worked out a general theory for the Force, and then I played with it. The more detail I went into, the more detracted from the concept I was trying to put forward. I wanted to take all religions, major religions and primitive religions, and come up with something they might have in common. It worked better as I got less specific...So the real essence was to try to deal with the Force but not to be too specific about it."

As George Lucas developed the idea further, the Force began to resemble the concept of *ki* in Japanese or *chi* in Chinese.

Obi-Wan Kenobi tells Luke in Star Wars that "The Force is what gives the Jedi his power. It's an energy field created by all living things. It surrounds us and penetrates us. It binds the galaxy together." In a similar vein, Yoda gives Luke his definition of the Force after the X-wing fighter has sunk in the swamp on Dagobah. Yoda states that the Force "a powerful ally it is. Life creates it, makes it grow. Its energy surrounds us and binds us. Luminous beings are we...not this crude matter. You must feel the Force around you. Here, between you...me...the tree...the rock...everywhere! Yes, even between the land and the ship!"

In this area the Force and the Tao are similar in many aspects. The Force surrounds us as does the Tao.

The great Tao flows everywhere
All things are born from it...
It is merged with all things
And hidden in their hearts

—Chapter 34

It flows through all things,
Inside and outside, and returns
To the origin of all things.

—Chapter 25

In the *Tao of Physics* Fritjof Capra explains how the Tao can be understood as and used to explain energy, as defined in modern physics. The Force as defined by Obi-Wan and Yoda is indeed an energy field. The Jedi get their strength from the Force and Yoda was able to lift the X-wing fighter out of the swamp with the aid of the Force because they are in harmony with the flow of the Force. Your strength comes from being in harmony with the Tao.

> *Open yourself to the Tao,*
> *Then trust your natural responses;*
> *And everything will fall into place.*
> —**Chapter 23**

> *She who is centered in the Tao*
> *Can go where she wishes, without danger.*
> *She perceives the universal harmony,*
> *Even amid great pain,*
> *Because she has found peace in her heart.*
> —**Chapter 35**

Yin and yang, the fundamental duality of the Tao that actually expresses the oneness of the Tao, is classically represented throughout the Star Wars series as the good side of the Force and the Dark side. The Force is neutral, it is how it is applied and how the characters flow with it and in it that determine their ultimate reality. When Yoda was instructing Luke on Dagobah in *Empire Strikes Back* he counseled Luke to "beware of the dark side. Anger...fear...aggression. The dark side of the Force are they. Easily they flow, quick to join you in a fight. If once you start down the dark path, forever will it dominate your destiny." The power of the dark side is, of course, personified by Darth Vader. He exhibits the power of the dark side when he chokes Motti from a distance while discussing the Death Star in *Star Wars*. He goes on to say, "Don't be too proud of this technological terror you've constructed. The ability to destroy a planet is insignificant next to the power of the Force."

The concept of yin and yang, as complementary pairs, with creative power is the essence of the good and dark side of the force. As complementary pairs, one cannot exist without the other. In fact, the presence of one creates the other.

> *The Tao doesn't take sides;*
> *It gives birth to both good and evil.*
> —**Chapter 5**

Although Darth Vader clearly went down the path to the dark side, the good in him had to still exist. You cannot have one without the other. Sometimes, no, most of the time, we become so focused on one side of a pair that we can no longer see the existence of the other. That is not the way of the Force and is definitely not the way of the Tao. The elimination of duality simply requires the recognition of the complementary pairs of yin and yang. Luke learned this lesson in *Return of the Jedi* when he looked for the good in his father, Darth Vader. Luke, speaking of Darth Vader while talking to the image of Obi-Wan, stated, "There is still good in him." Later in the same movie during the climactic fight between Luke and his father, between good and evil, the following exchange occurs.

LUKE: I know, Father.

VADER: So you have accepted the truth.

LUKE: I've accepted the truth that you were once

Anakin Skywalker, my father.

VADER: That name no longer has any meaning for me.

LUKE: It is the name of your true self. You've only forgotten. I know that there is good in you. The Emperor hasn't driven it from you fully.

Later in the battle, Luke once again tells his father that, "I feel the good in you…the conflict." It concludes with the Emperor about to kill Luke, after Luke had his lightsaber to the throat of Darth Vader but refused to kill him. At that time, Luke, still believing in the good in his father, cried out for help…"Father, please. Help me." Darth Vader then realizes the existence of the complementary pair and throws the Emperor to his death. Before his death, Vader says, "You were right. You were right about me." He finally recognized the good in himself. It had been there all of the time. All he needed to do was to acknowledge its existence for it to be made manifest. All we need to do is look…it is all there. There is no duality, just complementary pairs.

Another aspect of the Tao that is revealed in the Force is that of emptiness. Emptiness, as discussed in the Overview, includes the concept of void or nothingness from which all was created but it also includes the empty mind. This is best understood in the following Zen story.

> A noted philosopher goes to a Zen master for a teaching. After talking for a while the Zen master asks the philosopher if he would like tea and begins pouring. Soon the cup is filled and the tea begins to overflow onto the table and the floor. "What are you doing?" exclaims the philosopher in alarm. "You are like this cup," says the Zen master, "You come for information but you are completely full of ideas and beliefs. There is no room for anything more in your cup."

All too often, we are like the philosopher. We are full of ideas, preconceived notions and desires. We need to become empty in order to be receptive of the Tao and its flow.

> *The ancient masters*
> *Didn't try to educate the people,*
> *But kindly taught them to not-know.*
>
> *When they think that they know the answers,*
> *People are difficult to guide.*
> *When they know that they don't know,*
> *People can find their own way.*
> **—Chapter 65**

Yoda makes this clear to Luke on Dagobah during Luke's training.

> **LUKE**: But tell me why I can't…
>
> **YODA:** (interrupting) No, no, there is no why. Nothing more will I teach you today. Clear your mind of questions.

Later in the same teaching in response to the X-wing fighter sinking…

> **LUKE:** Master, moving stones around is one thing. This is totally different.
>
> **YODA:** No! No different! Only different in your mind. You must unlearn what you have learned.

It is clear that Yoda wants Luke to empty his mind so that he can learn the new things that he is presenting to Luke. The empty mind is fresh and open making it fertile ground for new possibilities. That is how the Tao works. It is not surprising, considering that George Lucas and his writing team were fascinated with old samurai movies, particularly *The Hidden*

Fortress by Akira Kurosawa. In those movies, as in Zen, one of the essential elements is the relationship between the master and his pupil. (Of note, Zen developed mostly as a "merger" of Taoism with Chinese Buddhism.) The paradox holds true—in order to be filled; you must first become empty.

As described in the Overview, the character for Tao is composed of two characters meaning a man running along a path. Throughout the Star Wars series the characters are forever mentioning following paths. This is highlighted in the following exchanges.

In *Star Wars* when Han initially refused to help in the attack on the Death Star…

> **LUKE:** Oh, it's Han! I don't know, I really thought he'd change his mind.

> **LEIA:** He's got to follow his own path. No one can choose it for him.

In *Star Wars* when Obi-Wan was leaving to take out the tractor beam and ultimately meet Darth Vader…

> **LUKE**: I want to go with you.

> **OBI-WAN:** Be patient, Luke. Stay and watch over the droids.

> **LUKE:** But he can —

> **OBI-WAN:** They must be delivered safely or other star systems will suffer the same fate as Alderaan. Your destiny lies along a different path from mine.

In *The Phantom Menace* when Anakin is told that he is free and can go with Qui-Gon…

> **QUI-GON:** Anakin, training to be a Jedi will not be an easy challenge. And if you succeed, it will be a hard life.

> **ANAKIN:** But it's what I want. What I've always dreamed about. Can I go mom?

> **QUI-GON:** This path has been placed before you, Annie; the choice to take it is yours alone.

In *The Phantom Menace* after the Jedi Council had initially told Qui-Gon that he could not teach Anakin the ways of the Jedi…

> **QUI-GON:** Anakin will become a Jedi…I promise you.

OBI-WAN: Don't defy the Council, Master…not again.

QUI-GON: I will do what I must.

OBI-WAN: Master, you could be sitting on the Council by now if you would just follow the code. They will not go along with you this time.

QUI-GON: You still have much to learn, my young apprentice.

What the young Obi-Wan has to learn is that the personal responsibility of following one's path is much more important than advancing along some external ranking system. Personal responsibility is key here. The path is put before you, but only you can choose to follow it. Qui-Gon and Obi-Wan both recognize that each person has their own path to follow in life. That path is ultimately the path of the Tao and is highly personal. As with any path, the key is to simply walk it and take it where it leads, experiencing life along the way.

CHAPTER THREE
ACCEPTANCE

In the midst of his ferocious battle for life and death with Darth Maul, Qui-Gon epitomizes all that is Tao, but mostly acceptance, which is one of the central tenets of Taoism. Darth Maul runs down a hallway, which is being bombarded by a series of pulsating energy rays. Qui-Gon follows after him. Darth Maul makes it through the hallway before the deadly rays close it off. Qui-Gon is one wall away from Darth Maul. Obi-Wan is just about to begin his trek down the hallway. Qui-Gon must wait until the next pulse to advance down the corridor. What Qui-Gon does next is indeed ultimate Tao. He does not pace impatiently as does his young apprentice Obi-Wan. He instead chooses to sit and meditate. He totally accepts the situation. He does not resist it. When the energy pulses fade, he immediately springs into action and the fight to the death continues.

This example could also be used to explain patience, *wu wei*, and present moment living. They are all related to acceptance.

The master sees things as they are,
Without trying to change them.
She lets them go their own way,
And resides at the center of the circle.
—Chapter 29

Acceptance is the ability to be with exactly what is—to hold the space for it, without trying to change it or transform it. It takes tremendous spiritual depth to keep including each moment as it arises, as Qui-Gon did while in the middle of the combat. We often, more times than not, want to interfere, to make it better, to fix it, or to transform the moment as opposed to accepting it for what it is. The modern concept is that I can make the world better, the way that I believe that the world should be.

Do you want to improve the world?
I don't think it can be done.

The world is sacred.
It can't be improved.
If you tamper with it, you'll ruin it.
If you treat it like an object, you'll lose it.
—Chapter 29

Things are as they are for a reason. Each moment is perfect in and of itself. Everything has its own place and function. That does not mean that we need to stop changing or trying to improve ourselves. It just means that we need to recognize what is there. Don't argue with what is, simply follow the path...simply follow the Tao.

It follows from the above that one of the key things to accept is the inevitability of change. Shmi discussed this with her son, Anakin, when he was afraid to leave with Qui-Gon.

SHMI: Son, my place is here. My future is here. It is time for you to let go...to let go of me. I cannot go with you.

ANAKIN: I want to stay with you. I don't want things to change.

SHMI: You can't stop change any more than you can stop the suns from setting. Listen to your feelings; Annie, you know what's right.

The only constant in life is change, therefore to resist is foolish, as foolish as trying to stop the sun(s) from rising.

If you realize that all things change,
There is nothing you will try to hold on to.
—**Chapter 74**

Interconnected concepts are those of detachment and contentment. In fact, they go hand-in-hand and spring from acceptance. In following the Tao, you have to relinquish your attachments to things being a certain way. This is detachment. It is crucial to remember that ideas can be things. Indeed, ideas can be some of the things to which we are most attached. This is best described by "disinterested interest." Disinterested means that your actions are not influenced by personal or selfish motives. You care about people, you care about things but you just don't mind the results that you get. A perfect example of this is Qui-Gon in his dealings with the Jedi Council in reference to his training young Anakin in the ways of the Jedi. He is told explicitly that he is not to train Anakin. Qui-Gon believes in his heart that Anakin is the Chosen One and tries to convince Mace Windu and Yoda that he should be allowed to train him.

> **YODA:** Our own counsel we will keep on who is ready. More to learn he has…
>
> **MACE WINDU:** Now is not the time for this…
>
> **YODA:** Young Skywalker's fate will be decided later.
>
> **QUI-GON:** I brought Anakin here; he must stay in my charge. He has nowhere else to go.

MACE WINDU: He is your ward, Qui-Gon…we will not dispute that.

YODA: Train him not. Take him with you, but train him not!

Qui-Gon earnestly believed that Anakin should be trained and lobbied hard for that result but he was not attached to the result. He was told no and told to go with the Queen and protect her. His response was:

QUI-GON: Your Highness, it is our pleasure to continue to serve and protect you.

AMIDALA: I welcome your help. Senator Palpatine fears the Federation means to destroy me.

QUI-GON: I promise you, I will not let that happen.

He cared but did not mind the result. He acted and then let go. He was detached.

We must allow our desires to naturally motivate our actions but not allow them to dominate us so much that we indulge ourselves in a futile attempt to control our uncontrollable lives. You must act without being attached to the results of the action. You have a right to the action but you do not have the right to the result. Similarly, you must have possessions without being possessed by them.

Fill your bowl to the brim
And it will spill.

*Keep sharpening your knife
And it will blunt.
Chase after money and security
And your heart will never unclench.
Care about people's approval
And you will be their prisoner.*

*Do your work, then step back.
The only path to serenity.*

—Chapter 9

Contentment flows from this. One way to define contentment is to accept what you have without the desire to have more. In actual fact, there is probably no greater disaster than discontentment. The only lasting satisfaction is that which is found in knowing when enough is enough.

*If you realize that you have enough,
You are truly rich.*

—Chapter 33

Be content with what you have;
Rejoice in the way things are.
When you realize there is nothing lacking,
The whole world belongs to you.

—**Chapter 44**

When you know when enough is enough, there will always be enough. This is a hard lesson to learn in our materialistic society where everything is geared to wanting more and more. Lieh Tzu, a Taoist who lived after Lao Tzu spoke to this over 2000 years ago:

> People believe they will find satisfaction in good food, expensive clothes, lively music, and exciting sex. But when they have all this they are still not satisfied. Having understood that happiness is not just about having one's material needs met, they desire prestige, fame, and recognition. Pulled by these glittering prizes and pushed by cultural pressure, people waste their short lives in pursuit of such goals. Their achievements may give them the illusion that they have gained something in their lives, but in reality they have lost a lot. They can no longer see, hear, feel, think, and act from their hearts. Social pressures from without dictate everything they do. They end up living the life others tell them to, not their own lives. Is this any different from being a slave or a prisoner?
>
> Having enough to eat...that is joy. Knowing when one is full...that is wisdom. Seek wisdom and know contentment.

When you practice acceptance, detachment and contentment (which of course are all interrelated) you can take life at face value and remove expectations.

The master's power is like this.
He lets all things come and go
Effortlessly, without desire.
He never expects results;
Thus he is never disappointed.
He is never disappointed;
Thus his spirit never grows old.

—**Chapter 55**

One of the simple truths of the world is that at the heart of all disappointment is an antecedent expectation. Eliminate expectations and all disappointments will disappear. How does one eliminate expectations? It is accomplished by practicing acceptance, detachment and contentment.

The one thing that many people, of all cultures, refuse to accept is death. Life and death are really the quintessential yin and yang, two sides of one ultimate reality. There is no life without death. Without death there could be no life. Death is the natural culmination of life that inevitably comes when it must. All three characters that were strong in the Force accept their death. Not only did they accept it, they knew the moment of its arrival. This has been true of all of the great spiritual leaders throughout history.

Obi-Wan in his battle with Darth Vader states, "You can't win, Darth. If you strike me down, I shall become more powerful than you can possibly imagine." When he sees Luke, he allows Vader to kill him. He accepted his death.

In *Return of the Jedi*, Luke returns to Dagobah to see Yoda. The following exchange occurs.

YODA: Hmm. That face you make? Look I so old to young eyes?

LUKE: No...of course not.

YODA: I do, yes, I do! Sick have I become. Old and weak. When nine hundred years old you reach, look as good you will not. Hmm? Soon I will rest. Yes, forever sleep. Earned it, I have.

LUKE: Master Yoda, you can't die.

YODA: Strong am I with the Force...but not that strong! Twilight is upon me, and soon night must fall. That is the way of things...the way of the Force.

Yoda could have easily said "That is the way of the Tao," for it most certainly is.

Darth Vader was indeed strong in the Force and he too knew the time of his approaching death and accepted it.

> **VADER:** Luke, help me take this mask off.

> **LUKE:** But you'll die.

> **VADER:** Nothing can stop that now. Just for once let me look on you with my own eyes.

> **ANAKIN (VADER WITH THE MASK OFF):** Now…go, my son. Leave me.

Accepting death is indeed the ultimate in acceptance and when carried to its logical conclusion, we die each moment ready to live the next. That is the key to present moment living.

Accept that you were born and that you will die and that the distance between is your personal path, Tao that is to be followed.

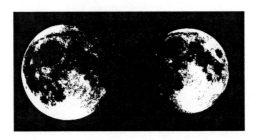

CHAPTER FOUR
PATIENCE

Star Wars could have easily been titled "Luke Needs Patience." It is clear that Luke had never read Chapter 67 in the *Tao Te Ching* that states:

> *I have just three things to teach:*
> *Simplicity, patience, compassion.*
> *These three are your greatest treasures.*

There are a plethora of examples in which Luke shows impatience. He desperately wanted off of Tatooine.

LUKE: It just isn't fair. Oh, Biggs is right. I'm never gonna get out of here!

THREEPIO: Is there anything that I might do to help?

LUKE: Well, not unless you can alter time, speed up the harvest, or teleport me off this rock!

THREEPIO: I don't think so, sir. I'm only a droid and not very knowledgeable about such things. Not on this planet, anyway. As a matter of fact, I'm not even sure which planet I'm on.

LUKE: Well, if there's a bright center to the universe, you're on the planet that it's farthest from.

Later in *Star Wars* in a discussion with his uncle:

LUKE: I think those new droids are going to work out fine. In fact, I, uh, was also thinking about our agreement, about me staying on another season. And if these new droids do work out, I want to transmit my application to the Academy this year.

OWEN: You mean the next semester before the harvest?

LUKE: Sure. There's more than enough droids.

OWEN: Harvest is when I need you the most. It's only one season more. This year we'll make enough money on the harvest that I'll be able to hire some more hands. And then you can go to the Academy next year. You must understand that I need you here, Luke.

LUKE: But it's a whole 'nother year.

OWEN: Look, it's only one more season.

LUKE: Yeah, that's what you said last year when Biggs and Tank left.

AUNT BERU: Where are you going?

LUKE: It looks like I'm going nowhere. I have to go finish cleaning those droids.

These are not only classic examples of impatience but show how patience, or the lack thereof, is related to acceptance.

> *...Patient with both friends and enemies,*
> *you accord with the way things are.*
>
> **—Chapter 67**

Luke did not accept his situation in life and was therefore was very impatient waiting for a change to occur. Patience flows from acceptance. And just as you first have to accept yourself and then the situation in which you find yourself, you first must be patient with yourself. Only then can you be patient with the situation. It is clear that all of the tenets of the Tao are indeed interconnected and mutually flow into and from one another.

One of the most important benefits of having patience is that it allows you to learn...to be taught. As a point in fact, Yoda told Obi-Wan on Dagobah, speaking of Luke, "I cannot teach him. The boy has no patience." Nothing worth knowing is learned quickly. How long does it take to achieve your black belt in the martial arts? How long does it take to become a concert pianist? How long does it take to become a skilled surgeon? It takes time and time requires patience. Moreover, having patience is a skill and, therefore, it too takes time to learn. Luke is told over and over again that he needs patience. Yet, even after being immersed in serious training with the master Yoda on Dagobah, Luke still has not learned patience. The following exchange occurs after Luke has a vision about Han and Leia being in danger on the Cloud City.

YODA: Luke! You must complete your training.

LUKE: I can't keep the vision out of my head. They're my friends. I've got to help them.

YODA: You must not go!

LUKE: But Han and Leia will die if I don't.

OBI-WAN: You don't know that. Even Yoda cannot

see their fate.

LUKE: But I can help them! I feel the Force.

OBI-WAN: But you cannot control it. This is a dangerous time for you, when you will be tempted by the dark side of the Force.

YODA: Yes, yes. To Obi-Wan you listen. The cave. Remember your failure at the cave!

LUKE: But I've learned so much since then, Master Yoda. I promise to return and finish what I have begun. You have my word.

Luke ignores his mentors' plea for patience and leaves for Cloud City. It takes time to learn patience, even with the best of mentors. Remember this well, as you proceed on your path to patience. This conversation also alludes to a related issue, that of perseverance. If, as stated above, it takes a long time to learn anything that is truly worthwhile, then it follows that it will take perseverance and commitment to the task at hand in order to complete it. Yoda was concerned that Luke not only lacked patience but lacked persistence. That is why he was hesitant in taking him on as a student.

YODA: (sighing) Will he finish what he begins?

That is why Luke said that he would return, he was aware of Yoda's concern. Patience and perseverance work together to yield results. You need both. Have the patience and persistence to complete what you begin, that alone is discipline and will lead to success.

If Luke is the epitome of impatience, which he is, then Qui-Gon is a pillar of patience. He not only speaks of patience but he puts patience into action. Is this another paradox of the Tao…patience and action together? Perhaps, but in actual fact patience can lead to the proper action.

> *Do you have the patience to wait*
> *Till your mud settles and the water is clear?*
> *Can you remain unmoving*
> *Till the right action arises by itself?*
> **—Chapter 15**

Thus, many times it is necessary to wait until the proper conditions arise and then the proper action is obvious. This is related to *wu wei*, to be discussed more fully in Chapter 6. Qui-Gon perfectly illustrates active patience many times.

When talking to Obi-Wan about selling things from the ship in order to purchase the hyperdrive generator…

> **QUI-GON:** …Obi-Wan, you're sure there isn't anything of value left on board?
>
> **OBI-WON:** A few containers of supplies, the Queen's wardrobe, maybe. Not enough for you to barter with. Not in the amounts you're talking about.
>
> **QUI-GON:** All right. Another solution will present itself. I'll check back.

That is actively practicing patience.

After his first encounter with Darth Maul on the surface of Tatooine...

> **ANAKIN:** Do you think he'll follow us?
>
> **QUI-GON:** We'll be safe enough once we're in hyper-space, but I have no doubt he knows our destination.
>
> **ANAKIN:** What are we going to do about it?
>
> **QUI-GON:** We will be patient.

When there is harmony between your words and action, a powerful lesson can be taught because the student sees that the teacher is indeed genuine. This needs to be remembered as you look for a teacher, but equally important, as you teach, especially those who are younger than you.

When explaining Midi-chlorians to Anakin...

> **ANAKIN:** Symbionts?

QUI-GON: Life forms living together for mutual advantage. Without the midi-chlorians, life could not exist, and we would have no knowledge of the Force. They continually speak to you, telling you the will of the Force.

ANAKIN: They do??

QUI-GON: When you learn to quiet your mind, you will hear them speaking to you.

ANAKIN: I don't understand.

QUI-GON: With time and training, Annie...you will.

He could have said, "With patience and persistence, you will."

One word that can be used to sum up Qui-Gon in relation to patience is equanimity. Various dictionaries define it as evenness of mind, remaining calm and undisturbed, especially under stress. It is both the source of harmonious action as well as being poised and centered in the midst of activity. The essence of Chapter 15 in the *Tao Te Ching* quoted above is, indeed equanimity. Actively practice equanimity.

The Force, as the Tao, is all-inclusive. It follows logically that if patience is important on the "good" side then it will be an important quality on the dark side.

In *Return of the Jedi...*

VADER: The Death Star will be completed on schedule.

EMPEROR: You have done well, Lord Vader. And now I sense you wish to continue your search for young Skywalker.

VADER: Yes, my master.

EMPEROR: Patience, my friend. In time he will seek you out.

That is the beauty of the Tao and the concept of yin and yang. It creates all and as complementary pairs, everything exists in us. All that we need to do is to be aware of the path…and walk it.

CHAPTER FIVE
UNCARVED BLOCK...P'U

It is no coincidence that the character who gives us the best insight into *P'u*, uncarved block, is a child. It is young Anakin Skywalker in *The Phantom Menace*. All great spiritual traditions emphasize the importance of having childlike characteristics in order to reach the pinnacle of the spiritual journey. Jesus stressed the importance in Matthew 18:3 when He said, "I tell you the truth, unless you change and become like little children, you will never enter the Kingdom of Heaven." The Tao is no different.

> *He who is in harmony with the Tao*
> *Is like a newborn child.*

—Chapter 55

Annie, as his mother and Qui-Gon were fond of calling him, was strong in the Force. Qui-Gon in talking with Shmi stated, "The Force is unusually strong with him, that much is clear." That is his natural state. That is *P'u*. It means that all things, especially people, in their original nature and simplicity contain their own natural power. Obviously this principle, as with the other principles and tenets, is related to others. In this case, *P'u* is related to simplicity and *Te*. As *Te* is the innate power and virtue that exists in all beings it is logical that *P'u* springs forth from this.

The natural state of man is as an uncarved block of wood or stone. It is ready to be molded.

The master views the parts with compassion,
Because he understands the whole.
His constant practice is humility.

He doesn't glitter like a jewel
But lets himself be shaped by the Tao,
As rugged and common as a stone.
—Chapter 39

The Tao is the sculptor and we are the clay. By being in harmony with the Tao we are molded and shaped based on our innate qualities and thus flow with the Tao. This is different from the western man who sees himself as a finished product molded, if you will, by himself through his efforts and actions. The western man is a finished work of art, and how often does a marble sculpture change, unless it is through decay?

Annie is ready to be molded but the path that he takes is up to him and the teaching that he receives. Just as a seed contains all that is needed for life to become a flower, so to the child is complete in its natural state but still needs to grow. If you put a seed in bad soil and don't give it enough water, then it will not grow. It still had all the requisites to become a flower but it was not tended to well. The same holds true for children and adults for that matter. People need teachers. The old Chinese saying is that when the student is ready the teacher will come. The teacher is the corollary to *P'u*, allowing the completeness of the seed that is within all of us to grow.

The master leads
By emptying people's minds
And filling their cores,
By weakening their ambition
And toughening their resolve.
He helps people lose everything
They know, everything they desire,
And creates confusion
In those who think that they know.
—Chapter 3

The goal of the teacher is to empty the student's mind of concepts, judgments, and desires thus returning them to a state of childlike simplicity.

Although Luke and Yoda on Dagobah was a classic master-student relationship, the relationship between Qui-Gon and Anakin is archetypal. Annie was ready for his teacher...

> **SHMI:** Is he to become a Jedi?

> **QUI-GON:** Our meeting was not a coincidence. Nothing happens by accident.

The essence of the master-student relationship is learning through observation. This is exemplified through the Chinese character *jian* that literally translates "to see."

It means that without observation, learning is impossible. After the Jedi Council told Qui-Gon that he could not take Anakin on as his formal apprentice...

> **ANAKIN:** Master Qui-Gon, sir, I do not wish to be a problem.

QUI-GON: You won't be, Annie…I'm not allowed to train you, so I want you to watch me and be mindful…always remember, your focus determines your reality. Stay close to me and you will be safe.

In this method of teaching, exemplified by Qui-Gon, the teacher trusts the student to see and trusts the student's perceptions. This is because the master trusts the Tao. Because the master was in harmony with the Tao, by simply observing the master as they traveled, the student would see Tao.

Remember *P'u*, your natural innate seed that is complete. Simply open your eyes and trust what you see.

> *(the master) what he desires is non-desire;*
> *what he learns is to unlearn.*
> *He simply reminds people*
> *Of who they have always been.*
> *He cares about nothing but the Tao.*
> *Thus he can care for all things.*
>
> **—Chapter 64**

CHAPTER SIX
WU WEI

If acceptance is the central tenet of the Tao, then *wu wei* is the cardinal tenet. As discussed in the Overview, it is perhaps the most misunderstood of all of the concepts in the Tao. Misunderstood mostly because it is diametrically opposed to most modern Western thoughts of action, competition, assertiveness, and interference in the flow of events. In short, Western Man wants to exert his will not only over other people but also over nature itself. This is not the way of the Tao.

> *The Tao never does anything,*
> *Yet through it all things are done.*
> **—Chapter 37**

Wu wei is not non-action but effortless action. It is action without doing, causing or making. It is action without meddlesome, contentious or egotistical exertion. *Wu wei* is the effortless action that results from combining your inner nature (*P'u* and Te) with the natural laws operating around you. In short, it is being in harmony with the Tao. It is harmonious action and therefore is effortless. It is going with the spontaneous flow of Tao with the absence of human willful efforts. The prerequisite for this is to feel the Tao. You cannot harmonize with the Tao if you don't feel it or are not aware of its presence.

Throughout the Star Wars series those strong in the Force are constantly talking about feeling the Force.

In *Star Wars* when Obi-Wan asks Luke to come with him...

> **OBI-WAN:** You must do what you feel is right, of course.

Later, when Luke is learning how to use the lightsaber against the remote...

> **OBI-WAN:** Remember, a Jedi can feel the Force flowing through him.

> **LUKE:** You mean it controls your actions?

> **OBI-WAN:** Partially.

In *The Empire Strikes Back* Yoda is constantly admonishing Luke to feel the Force during his training on Dagobah...

> **YODA:** Run! Yes. A Jedi's strength flows from the Force.

When you are aware of the Tao and feel it, you can flow with it, and the right action appears for itself, spontaneously. This is the essence of *wu wei*.

> *Can you remain unmoving*
> *Till the right action arises by itself?*
>
> **—Chapter 15**

This relates *wu wei* to patience. You wait…you feel…you harmonize and the right action appears. That is *wu wei*. This type of patience can best be described as vigilance. This is seen throughout the animal kingdom. The tiger in a crouch waiting to pounce…the crane standing on one leg waiting for the fish to swim by…the python lying in wait for the prey to pass by. What do all of these have in common? Vigilance, not just mere waiting, but waiting for the proper time to act. It also encompasses not only being in the right place at the right time but ready to act. Act in harmony with the Tao.

Related to feeling the Tao, as alluded to above, is being aware of the Tao. Awareness or mindfulness is key to most Eastern philosophies, especially Buddhism, Zen and Taoism.

While training on Dagobah, Yoda was forever telling Luke to focus in order to feel the Force…

> **YODA:** Feel it. (Luke becomes distracted by Artoo's frantic beeping. Luke loses his balance.)

> **YODA:** Concentrate!

Later, Luke is standing upside down, but his face shows less strain and more concentration than before. Yoda stands beside him.

> **YODA:** Concentrate. (Equipment slowly rises into the air.)

> **YODA:** Feel the Force flow. Yes.

In *The Phantom Menace*, the very first scene has Qui-Gon telling Obi-Wan to, "…be mindful of the living Force." You feel the Tao. You are aware of the Tao. From this flows your strength, the strength of spontaneous, harmonious action…*wu wei*.

Effortless action does not come with egotistical forcing of things. It does not come with knowledge, for knowledge tries to figure things out. Knowledge leads to cleverness, which tries to devise better ways.

> *Do you want to improve the world?*
> *I don't think it can be done.*
> **—Chapter 29**

Wu wei doesn't think. As the peerless martial artist Bruce Lee said in *Enter the Dragon* when instructing the young student, "Don't think…Feel."

Obviously, effortless action requires no effort. The ego forces. The ego imposes. Humans try. On Dagobah...

LUKE: I'll give it a try.

YODA: No! Try not. Do. Or do not. There is no try.

Trying is not the way nature functions. The earth doesn't try to orbit the sun. The seed doesn't try to grow into a tree. Nature functions with effortless ease, invariably taking the path of least resistance. *Wu wei* doesn't try, it just does. And when it does, it doesn't appear to do much of anything but things get done. Trying too hard leads to failure.

In order to practice *wu wei*, you have to let go. This is what Obi-Wan told Luke in *Star Wars* as he was attempting to release the laser torpedoes at the Death Star. Luke was attempting to use his instrumentation to find the target and to determine the release point.

OBI-WAN: Use the Force, Luke.

Luke looks up, then starts to look back into the targeting device. He has second thoughts.

OBI-WAN: Let go, Luke.

You have to let go and trust the Tao. That is the path to harmonious action, by letting go and allowing things to take their own course.

> *True mastery can be gained*
> *By letting things go their own way.*
> *It can't be gained by interfering.*
> **—Chapter 48**

There is one more element of letting go that is of prime importance. That is to let go of desire, which is just another way of defining acceptance. Of course the central tenet of Taoism, acceptance, will be intimately related to the cardinal tenet, *wu wei*. Lack of acceptance with the way things are, desire, is at the root of every action, interference or assertion.

The Tao never does anything,
Yet through it all things are done.

If powerful men and women
Could center themselves in it (They can!)
The whole world would be transformed
By itself, in its natural rhythms.
People would be content
With their simple, everyday lives,
In harmony, and free of desire.

When there is no desire,
All things are at peace.

—Chapter 37

When you have acceptance and act in harmony with the Tao, you can put aside personal priorities in order to fulfill the demands of the time, *wu wei*, harmonious action. *Wu wei* is one of the greatest skills, use it well…use it often.

CHAPTER SEVEN
SIMPLICITY

Yoda is the picture of simplicity, so much so, that he could have written the following:

> *I have just three things to teach:*
> *Simplicity, patience, compassion.*
> *These three are your greatest treasures.*
> *...Simple in actions and in thoughts,*
> *you return to the source of being.*
>
> **—Chapter 67**

Being that he was 900 years old when he died, perhaps Yoda did write Chapter 67!

In *The Empire Strikes Back*, Luke crashes into the swamp on Dagobah. He is looking for Yoda, the Jedi Master.

LUKE: Now all I got to do is find this Yoda…if he even exists. It's really a strange place to find a Jedi Master. Still…there's something familiar about this place. I don't know…I feel like…

YODA: Feel like what?

LUKE: Like we're being watched!

YODA: Away put your weapon! I mean you no harm. I am wondering, why are you here?

LUKE: I'm looking for someone.

YODA: Looking? Found someone, you have, I would say, hmmm?

LUKE: Right.

YODA: Help you I can. Yes, mmmm.

LUKE: I don't think so. I'm looking for a great warrior.

YODA: Ahhh! A great warrior. Wars not make one great.

Later…

LUKE: Don't do that. Ohh…you're making a mess. Hey, give me that!

YODA: Mine! Or I will help you not.

LUKE: I don't want your help. I want my lamp back. I'm gonna need to get out of this slimy mud hole.

YODA: Mudhole? Slimy? My home this is.

Yoda exhibits many of the qualities of simplicity in this meeting. If there is one thing that epitomizes simplicity, it is water.

The supreme good is like water,
Which nourishes all things without trying to.
It is content with the low places that people disdain.
Thus it is like the Tao.
—Chapter 8

This is Yoda. He maintains his simplicity despite being a renowned master. Perhaps it is his simplicity that makes him great. Chapter 8 in the *Tao Te Ching* goes on to give explicit advice on how to live like water, that is, to maintain a simple life.

In dwelling, live close to the ground

Luke described Dagobah as a slimy mudhole but to Yoda it was home. Close to the ground and simple. When you are simple in your dwelling you are closer to your original self...*P'u.* Of course, all qualities of Tao are interrelated, thus simplicity is no different. Simplicity springs from *P'u* or does *P'u* flow from simplicity? Does it really matter? Perhaps not.

In thinking, keep to the simple.

One of the things that demonstrate thinking is the ability to communicate clearly in a concise manner. Although Yoda's speech pattern is often inverted, it is always clear and concise. His thought pattern is simple and logical, aware of the obvious.

> **LUKE:** I'm looking for someone.

> **YODA:** Looking? Found someone, you have, I would say, hmmm?

This is a classic example of simple, straightforward thinking.

> *In conflict, be fair and generous.*

Yoda states that, "Wars not make one great." Taoism is essentially a pacifist philosophy, which is also realistic. Avoid war at all costs but if necessary use restraint.

> *Weapons are the tools of fear;*
> *A decent man will avoid them*
> *Except in the direst necessity*
> *And, if compelled, will use them*
> *Only with the utmost restraint.*
> *Peace is his highest value,*
> *If the peace has been shattered,*
> *How can he be content?*
> *His enemies are not demons,*
> *But human beings like himself.*
> *He doesn't wish them personal harm.*
> *Nor does he rejoice in victory.*
> *How could he rejoice in victory*
> *And delight in the slaughter of men?*

He enters a battle gravely,
With sorrow and with great compassion,
As if he were attending a funeral.

—Chapter 31

The man of Tao, the simple man, realizes that although war may be necessary, it does not make one great.

In governing, don't try to control

—Chapter 8

Throughout his encounters with Luke, Yoda leads Luke. He shows him examples. He makes him observe. Yoda never controls. Remember acceptance. Remember *wu wei*. The universe is always out of the control of your own personal, conscious self. Yoda knows this and puts it into practice, and so should you.

In work, do what you enjoy.

How can you do the same job for over 800 years and not enjoy it? Obviously Yoda enjoyed training those strong in the Force to become Jedi Knights. Confucius said, "That if you choose a job that you love, you will never have to work a day in your life."

In family life, be completely present

The Jedi were indeed Yoda's family. He was always there for them.

Again, Chapter 8 of the *Tao Te Ching* Lao Tzu gives instructions on how to live a simple life. Of note, the instructions themselves are simple. Imagine how your daily life would be if you put into action those six simple rules?

You would be content at work. You would be content at home. You would have fewer conflicts since you were not trying to control. You would have fewer arguments since your thinking was clear and concise.

> *When you are content to be simply yourself*
> *And don't compare or compete,*
> *Everyone will respect you.*
> **—Chapter 8**

> *Do your work, then step back.*
> *The only path to serenity.*
> **—Chapter 9**

To be simply ourselves is the greatest challenge but is one of the techniques that leads to true contentment.

One of the classic examples of simplicity is illustrated in the following story:

> One of the ancients of Tao, Zhuang Zi, was fishing when two imperial courtiers came to him. The emperor wanted Zhuang Zi to become a high official. It would be a true honor. Zhuang Zi said to the courtiers, "There is an ancient turtle shell in the imperial temple used by the national priests for divination. Do you think the turtle would rather be highly venerated or dragging its tail in the mud?" The officials replied, "We suppose that he would rather be dragging his tail in the mud." At that, Zhuang Zi burst out, "Go away then, and let me drag my tail in the mud!"

Zhuang Zi and the turtle both preferred their innate simplicity. Again illustrating the interrelatedness of simplicity and *P'u*. It also connects simplicity with acceptance. By simply acknowledging their true nature and their lot in life both Zhuang Zi and the turtle found contentment. That is the beauty of acceptance…it brings contentment.

The Tao never does anything,
Yet through it all things are done.

If powerful men and women
Could center themselves in it (They can!)
The whole world would be transformed
By itself, in its natural rhythms.
People would be content
With their simple, everyday lives,
In harmony, and free of desire.

When there is no desire,
All things are at peace.

—Chapter 37

This chapter in *Tao Te Ching* shows how simplicity, *P'u*, acceptance and *wu wei* flow from each other and are interconnected. Simplicity and *P'u* induce a state of desirelessness within you. From desirelessness, acceptance emanates which induces a state of serenity and contentment. All of this produces a person who sees no need to interfere with or exert the force of his will onto the world...*wu wei*.

You already have all that you need...on the inside. In *The Empire Strikes Back* when Luke was about to go into the cave on Dagobah...

YODA: That place...is strong with the dark side of the Force. A domain of evil it is. In you must go.

LUKE: What's in there?

YODA: Only what you take with you.

It is all present within you. That is a simple spiritual truth. Jesus states the same thing in Luke 17:20-21. Once, having been asked by the Pharisees when the kingdom of God would come, Jesus replied, "The kingdom of God does not come with your careful observation, nor will people say, 'Here it is,' or 'There it is,' because the kingdom of God is within you."

Life is to be kept simple—conserve energy, maintain your center, be content with what you have, and be content with who you are. Simply be yourself, all that you need is already there…on the inside.

CHAPTER EIGHT
HUMILITY

As it is in life, the Tao is replete with paradoxes. There is none greater than the fact that it is from humility that greatness arises. Qui-Gon, Obi-Wan and Yoda, all strong in the Force, display humility. They were all unpretentious. Yet, they were all great.

In *Star Wars*, Obi-Wan is the picture of humility when he met Luke in the wastelands of Tattooine where the Sandpeople lived. He was helpful without listing his qualifications. In fact, he was not even using his real name. He did not boast about being a Jedi. In Chapter Seven, on simplicity, we talked about how Yoda was the portrait of simplicity when he met Luke on Dagobah. As simplicity is linked to humility, that same encounter can be used to illustrate Yoda's humility. If there was ever a truly great Jedi master, then it was Yoda. Yet he did not brag about how great he was. As Obi-Wan before him, he did not even tell Luke his true identity.

The master, by residing in the Tao,
Sets an example for all beings.
Because he doesn't display himself,
People can see his light.
Because he has nothing to prove,
People can trust his words.

—Chapter 22

By being at one with the Tao, you have unity, balance and harmony. This frees you from selfish thoughts, words and deeds. You can practice humility. You have no motive to show off your accomplishments, justify your actions or to otherwise bring attention to yourself.

He who stands on tiptoe
Doesn't stand firm.
He who rushes ahead
Doesn't go far.
He who tries to shine
Dims his own light.
He who defines himself
Can't know who he really is.

—Chapter 24

Related to humility, indeed flowing from it is yielding. In fact,

Yielding is the way of the Tao.

—Chapter 40

There is strength in yielding. In *Star Wars* after the Millennium

Falcon was caught in a tractor beam and was about to boarded by the stormtroopers...

HAN: I'm going to have to shut down. But they're not going to get me without a fight!

OBI-WAN: You can't win. But there are alternatives to fighting.

Knowing how to yield is strength.
                                        —**Chapter 52**

A corollary to that is that knowing when to yield is strength. In *Star Wars*, Obi-Wan, the personification of humility and yielding drew his lightsaber to battle Darth Vader. The essence of yielding is therefore to know when and how to yield. Humility and compassion may be among the treasured virtues, but they are not always the most useful in a conflict. And as true realists, those who follow the Tao know that conflict is indeed inevitable. However, that does not lessen its evil. Therefore, as Obi-Wan illustrated, there are times to yield and times to act (note, however, that yielding is a conscious thought and an action). If you must act, then act to win but always prefer to live in peace.

A related concept is martial training. The Jedi, strong in and knowledgeable of the Force also were highly trained martial artists. They were trained in the "way of the lightsaber." *Wu*, in Chinese and *Bu*, in Japanese, mean to stop the sword. The sword, however, is not necessarily just to slay others, but to subdue the self. As O'Sensei, the founder of Aikido, stated, "True victory is victory over the self." The greatest taming of the martial is to tame one's character.

If there is one thing in the world that typifies humility and yielding, it is water.

Nothing in the world
Is as soft and yielding as water.
Yet for dissolving the hard and inflexible,
Nothing can surpass it.

—Chapter 78

Water is yielding however nothing is as mighty. Look at the Grand Canyon. Look at the power of a tsunami. Look at the potholes in your streets. How is this accomplished? Through humility and yielding. Water accumulates because it seeks the lower ground. It will not hesitate (as if something flowing with the Tao could ever hesitate…its actions are in harmony with the Tao and therefore always correct and timed appropriately) to go into deep ravines or dirty places. By doing this, more and more water comes together until the result is a force that none can resist. It is the same for us. It is only by being humble that we can become truly great.

The supreme good is like water,
Which nourishes all things without trying to.
It is content with the low places that people disdain.
Thus it is like the Tao.

—Chapter 8

The master doesn't try to be powerful;
Thus he is truly powerful.

—Chapter 38

It must be noted that this is not a false humility just to gain greatness. Humility flows from the Tao and its greatness. You are one with the Tao and therein emanates your power. You realize that you are not the doer separate from the world but one with the world. Your greatness comes to the fore naturally.

The master keeps her mind
Always at one with the Tao;
That is what gives her radiance.

—**Chapter 21**

With that, comes the need for even more humility.

When a country obtains great power,
It becomes like the sea:
All streams run downward into it.
The more powerful it grows,
The greater the need for humility.
Humility means trusting the Tao,
Thus never needing to be defensive.

—**Chapter 61**

Silence is a related concept and flows from humility. The first aspect of silence has to do with speech. In *The Phantom Menace*, when Qui-Gon first meets Jar Jar the following exchange occurs...

> **QUI-GON:** Are you brainless? You almost got us killed!

> **JAR JAR:** I spake.

> **QUI-GON:** The ability to speak does not make you intelligent.

We all know people who not only love to talk but talk too much. On closer self-examination, we may be one of them.

Express yourself completely,
Then keep quiet.
Be like the forces of nature:
When it blows, there is only wind;
When it rains, there is only rain;
When the clouds pass, the sun shines through.
—Chapter 23

If nature, with all of its power and fury, knows when to stop, then shouldn't we do the same? Say what you need to say and let that be sufficient. This is similar to right speech in Buddhism and when Jesus spoke about oaths in Luke 5:37 "Simply let your 'Yes' be 'Yes' your 'No,' 'No.'" Active practice of this aspect of silence not only flows from humility but leads to more humility and non-contention.

Wise men don't need to prove their point;
Men who need to prove their point aren't wise.
—Chapter 81

The second aspect of silence relates to the mind. The mind must be kept quiet. A quiet mind is in tune with the Tao. On Dagobah when Yoda was teaching Luke…

LUKE: But how am I to know the good side from the bad?

YODA: You will know. When you are calm, at peace.

Remember that the quiet mind is empty and therefore open to all possibilities. In *The Phantom Menace* when Anakin was confused over the nature of the midi-chlorians....

QUI-GON: They continually speak to you, telling you the will of the Force.

ANAKIN: They do??

QUI-GON: When you learn to quiet your mind, you will hear them speaking to you.

Empty your mind of all thoughts.
Let your heart be at peace.
Watch the turmoil of beings,
But contemplates their return
—Chapter 16

Quieting the mind is really the essence of meditation. You empty the mind to see the ultimate unity between you and all existence. That brings peace. That breeds patience. That brings acceptance. That allows *wu wei* to exist. Quieting the mind allows you to be still so that you can reflect upon the world as it really is, not as you think it should be. The empty mind does not grasp. The empty mind does not reject. It is like a mirror. A mirror will reflect all things perfectly. It never refuses to show a thing. Moreover, it does not retain the thing after it is gone. That is the quiet, empty mind. The surface of the pond cannot reflect the moon until it has become still. Still the mind and know peace because you will be in harmony with the Tao.

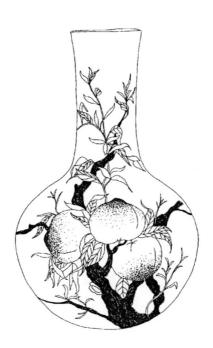

CHAPTER NINE
LIFE EXPERIENCE

All of the other tenets of the Tao that have been covered deal with how to live in this world, not as a hermit on a mountain. Life is the proving ground of the Tao, where you put your knowledge of the tenets into action. The Tao is life. Life is the ultimate school, however, it teaches in a different fashion than traditional school. In class, you receive the lesson, study it and then there is a test. Life does the reverse. You have the test and then you have to be awake and open to the lesson.

When Qui-Gon and Obi-Won first land on Naboo, they encounter troops firing upon them and they need to use their lightsabers. Obi-Won's lightsaber does not ignite.

OBI-WAN: Sorry, Master, the water fried my weapon.

QUI-GON: (Inspects the burnt lightsaber handle) You

forgot to turn off your power again, didn't you?

(Obi-Wan nods sheepishly)

QUI-GON: It won't take long to recharge, but this is a lesson I hope you've learned, my young Padawan.

OBI-WAN: Yes, Master.

This shows that life gives the test first. It takes awareness to learn the lesson from the test. Obi-Won was fortunate to have a good teacher to point the lesson out to him after the test. This points out the value of having a good teacher but we may not always have one. Even if we have one, we may not listen. Hear what Yoda told Luke during Luke's training on Dagobah after the X-wing fighter has completely sunk into the swamp.

LUKE: Oh, no. We'll never get out now.

YODA: So certain are you. Always with you it cannot be done. Hear you nothing that I say?

So it is not just enough to have a teacher, you must hear and listen. It is not just enough to live, you must be aware. Most of the time we are not fortunate enough to have a teacher, especially one skilled in practicing the Tao. It is during those times that we have to be open and aware. That is okay, however. The reason is that there comes a point beyond which teaching cannot provide for you. Only direct experience can give you the final instruction that you need. That means learning from nature and learning from yourself. In each and every life experience there is a chance to learn. There is a Chinese maxim about a seeker who climbs a very high mountain to ask the hermit sage about the meaning of life.

Seeker: What is the most important aspect of one's life?

Sage: Experience

Seeker: How do you get experience?

Sage: Good judgment

Seeker: How do you get good judgment?

Sage: Bad judgment

Failure is an opportunity.
If you blame someone else,
There is no end to the blame.

Therefore the master
Fulfills her own obligations
And corrects her own mistakes.
She does what she needs to do
And demands nothing of others.

—Chapter 79

Life is full of examples of learning from one's failures or defeats. There is a paradox here as well, however.

> *Success is as dangerous as failure.*
> **—Chapter 13**

Paul "Bear" Bryant, the famous college football coach, said, "Others study the films of the games that they have lost to see what they did wrong. I study the films of the games that we won to see what we did right." That is sound advice, for every life experience is indeed a learning opportunity, however it points to the problem of success. The ego feeds on success and causes one to deviate from humility, to become selfish and to deviate from the Tao. The corollary of this is the fear of losing success or favor. They work together to inflate the ego or to avoid deflating it. That is not the way of the Tao. The way of the Tao is balance, moderation, equanimity and harmony.

> *What does it mean that success is as dangerous as failure?*
> *Whether you go up the ladder or down it,*
> *Your position is shaky.*
> *When you stand with your two feet on the ground,*
> *You will always keep your balance.*
> **—Chapter 13**

The key is to keep both feet on the ground, maintaining your balance whether you are succeeding or failing. Humility, simplicity, patience, acceptance and *wu wei* are most helpful in allowing you to maintain this balance, in fact, they are essential.

In *The Phantom Menace* at times it seemed as if Jar Jar was more trouble than he was worth. However, anyone or anything can be useful in the proper situation. It was Jar Jar who helped navigate Qui-Gon and Obi-Won out of the underwater city to reach the Queen. By being open to the flow of life's lesson, to the path that you are on, you can pick up on what is useful at that time and what is not. You then go with the flow, in harmony...*wu wei*.

> *A good traveler has no fixed plans*
> *And is not intent upon arriving.*
> *A good artist lets his intuition*
> *Lead him wherever it wants.*
> *A good scientist has freed himself of concepts*
> *And keeps his mind open to what is.*
>
> *Thus the master is available to all people*
> *And doesn't reject anyone.*
> *He is ready to use all situations*
> *And doesn't waste anything.*
> *This is called embodying the light.*
>
> *What is a good man but a bad man's teacher?*
> *What is a bad man but a good man's job?*
> *If you don't understand this, you will get lost,*
> *However intelligent you are.*
> *It is the great secret.*
>
> **—Chapter 27**

Again, this seems paradoxical. However it is blatantly unwise to reject anyone because he is "bad." The reason is that a "bad" man can turn good and even serve some good purpose. From the doings of this so-called bad man and their consequences, one may learn a lesson or even find a way to turn bad into good. You can learn from anyone or anything. You should therefore honor the teacher and love the lesson. Remember it was Jar Jar who helped come up with the plan in the end that led to victory. This makes logical sense but is not followed by most people. We limit our teachers, thus limiting our lessons and stunting our growth.

Related to learning from everyone is that everything has its time and place. Almost any action can be right if it takes place in the proper time and place, under the proper circumstances. Qui-Gon illustrated this when trying to barter for the new hyperdrive generator.

> **PADME:** These junk dealers must have a weakness of some kind.

> **SHMI:** Gambling. Everything here revolves around betting on those awful races.

> **QUI-GON:** Podracing…Greed can be a powerful ally…if it's used properly.

Even something as "bad" as greed can be useful. Even something as abhorrent as death can be legitimately justified in the proper circumstances.

> *There is a time for being ahead,*
> *A time for being behind;*
> *A time for being in motion,*
> *A time for being at rest;*
> *A time for being vigorous,*
> *A time for being exhausted;*
> *A time for being safe,*
> *A time for being in danger.*

—Chapter 29

This is very similar to Ecclesiastes 3:1-8, which says:

> *There is a time for everything, and a season for every activity under heaven:*
> *A time to be born and a time to die,*
> *A time to plant and a time to uproot,*
> *A time to tear down and a time to build,*
> *A time to weep and a time to laugh,*
> *A time to mourn and a time to dance,*
> *A time to scatter stones and a time to gather them,*
> *A time to embrace and a time to refrain,*
> *A time to search and a time to give up,*
> *A time to keep and a time to throw away,*
> *A time to tear and a time to mend,*
> *A time to be silent and a time to speak,*
> *A time to love and a time to hate,*
> *A time for war and a time for peace.*

One of the truisms in life is that everything happens for a reason. We might not know the reason or we might interpret it erroneously. That can happen because we are not mindful of the situation or we may have the wrong perspective. In *Return of the Jedi*, Luke asks Obi-Wan a question.

> **LUKE:** Why didn't you tell me? You told me Vader betrayed and murdered my father.

> **OBI-WAN:** Your father was seduced by the dark side of the Force. He ceased to be Anakin Skywalker and became Darth Vader. When that happened, the good man who was your father was destroyed. So what I told you was true…from a certain point of view!

> **LUKE:** A certain point of view!

> **OBI-WAN:** Luke, you're going to find that many of the truths we cling to depend greatly on our point of view.

How one's perspective can color one's view of the world is also illustrated by the following story.

There was a man who was the leader of an Alcoholic Anonymous group. He wanted to prove to them once and for all that alcohol was indeed bad. While standing in front of the group, he had two flasks. One was filled with pure water and the other with pure alcohol. He dropped a worm in the flask of pure water. The worm swam merrily around. He then took the worm and placed it into the flask containing pure alcohol. Right in front of their eyes, the worm disintegrated. The man yelled, "See! See! What does that prove to you about alcohol?" A voice from the back yelled, "It proves that if you drink alcohol you will never have worms."

Your perceptions, preconceived notions and viewpoint color how you interpret the world. All meaning in life is arbitrary; it is we who assign meaning. Remember, everything happens for a reason. After Anakin won the Podrace he was given his freedom.

> **SHMI:** Now you can make your dreams come true, Annie. You're free! Will you take him with you? Is he to become a Jedi?

> **QUI-GON:** Our meeting was not a coincidence. Nothing happens by accident.

In essence, what Qui-Gon was describing is synchronicity. Although it has existed forever, it was first described by the noted psychologist Carl Jung. He defined synchronicity, as the acausal connecting principle that manifests itself through meaningful coincidences that cannot be explained by simple cause and effect. (It is perhaps no coincidence that he expounded on this principle in the introduction of the first major non-Chinese translation of the *I Ching* in the early part of the twentieth century.) How does one discern these meaningful coincidences from the myriad of things that happen to us each day? The Tao instructs us to be open to the world. To have an empty mind and to experience the world as it is. Each day we experience a plethora of phenomena and it is up to us to see them with an open mind and derive their true meaning.

There is value in each life experience…yes. And the only thing constant is change. Acceptance is one of the cornerstones of the

Tao. So how does one know when to change? When is change going with the flow of the Tao and when is it going against it?

If you realize that all things change,
There is nothing you will try to hold on to.
If you aren't afraid of dying,
There is nothing you can't achieve.

Trying to control the future
Is like trying to take the master carpenter's place.
When you handle the master carpenter's tools,
Chances are that you'll cut your hand.
—Chapter 74

When things become difficult, when obstacles mount, when troubles arise, it is not the time to exert more force. It is time to be quiet, still and empty until the proper action comes. That is when it is time to change. We cannot always know what is good or bad about a situation. We cannot control or predict the future. So we need to have patience and allow the flow of the Tao to signal the best possible action. This is illustrated beautifully in the following classic story from the Huai Nan Tzu.

A poor farmer's horse ran off into the country of the barbarians. All his neighbors offered their condolences, but the man said, "How do you know that this isn't good fortune?" After a few months the horse returned with a barbarian horse of excellent stock. All his neighbors offered their congratulations, but the man said, "How do you know that this isn't a disaster?" The two horses bred, and the family became rich in fine horses. The farmer's son spent much of his time riding them; one day he fell off and broke his hipbone. All his neighbors offered the farmer their condolences, but the father said, "How do you know that this isn't good fortune?"

Another year passed, and the barbarians invaded the frontier. All the able-bodied young men were conscripted, and nine-tenths of them died in the war. Thus good fortune can be disaster and vice versa. Who can tell how events will be transformed?

Acceptance. Simplicity. Humility. *P'u*. Patience. *Wu wei*. They are all tenets of the Tao. Knowledge of them will serve you well. However, there is no understanding without practice. You must experience life, that is the ultimate value of the Tao. It is not enough to have the philosophy of the Tao. One must live it.

CHAPTER TEN
PRESENT MOMENT LIVING

What is the purpose of life? Why am I here? I would guess that those questions were some of the first questions that thinking man asked. And you know, we are still asking them today and searching for the answer. I believe that quest, in part, is a reason for the success of the Star War series. Obviously, there are as many answers to these questions as there are religions and philosophies.

We can get a glimpse at the answer by looking at death. Another seeming paradox, looking at death to find the answer to the purpose of life. Allow me to simply state the main difference between Taoism and Western religions. The key difference is their view on death. In the West, death is the beginning of the afterlife. If you have lived your life according to certain precepts then you will get to the afterlife in good standing. Thus the purpose of life is to follow the precepts and be rewarded with a wonderful afterlife. In Taoism, death is just a part of life. In fact, as previously discussed, life and death are complementary pairs, two sides of the same coin, each defining the other. When you accept death you value each moment and choose to be aware in that moment and to act accordingly. Thus, the focus is on this life, not the afterlife. The key is this life, with how to live in each present moment being of utmost importance. As discussed in the chapter on acceptance, all three characters that were strong in the Force accepted their death at the appropriate time. They knew that they had lived well.

> **YODA:** Soon I will rest. Yes, forever sleep. Earned it
> I have.

No mention of an afterlife here. No regrets here. Just comfort in knowing that he had lived a good life. A life that consists of a stream of connected moments that need to be simply lived. Just as it is for us. This makes logical sense in that the Tao is indeed a path that needs to be walked.

The purpose of life...to live each moment to the fullest. The very act of being fully present in our lives is spirituality enough, for being present is to acknowledge that everything is spiritual.

> *The master gives himself up*
> *To whatever the moment brings.*
> *He knows that he is going to die,*
> *And he has nothing left to hold on to:*
> *No illusions in his mind,*
> *No resistances in his body.*
> *He doesn't think about his actions;*
> *They flow from the core of his being.*
> *He holds nothing back from life;*
> *Therefore he is ready for death,*
> *As a man is ready for sleep*
> *After a good day's work.*
>
> **—Chapter 50**

It could be argued that luck and fate get in the way of living each moment to the fullest. That is not the case, for in reality neither of them exists, especially in the sense that we normally think of them. In *Star Wars*, the following exchange occurred while Obi-Wan was teaching Luke the ways of the Force while practicing with his lightsaber against the remote...

OBI-WAN: You see, you can do it.

HAN: I call it luck.

OBI-WAN: In my experience, there is no such thing as luck.

It has been said as one gets better training, more knowledge, and more practice, that their luck will improve. As with every-thing else, luck depends on you, what you have on the inside and what you do.

As our luck depends on us, so too, our fate. Each time we act, we generate a chain of events that is tied to us completely. That is fate. In essence, we create our own fate by the choices that we make. On Dagobah, after Luke saw a vision of Han and Leia in danger, he wanted to end his training and go help them.

LUKE: I've got to go to them.

YODA: Decide you must how to serve them best. If you leave now, help them you could. But you would destroy all for which they have fought and suffered.

Luke's "fate" is determined by his choice. Fate is simply the consequences of our actions. A constantly fluid set of limita-tions created by the intentions of our decisions and our oppor-tunities. We are personally responsible for the vast majority of our fate. That is a frightening thought…personal responsibili-ty. Although many of us claim to not like being told what to do, making our own choices can be paralyzing. One of the things that leads to paralysis is regret, should I have made another choice? When you walk a path, you should not regret another path not taken. You have to accept that fact that you cannot travel on one path while walking another. If you go to one des-tination, then it is inevitable that you will miss others. If you have been fully involved with your own life and have been making your own choices, in harmony with the Tao, there will be no reason for regret.

In the West we have been taught that there are evil forces out there that can control you, just as there are good forces. We are to seek the good ones and they will protect us. The Tao says something different. Good and evil are both within us and it is by our actions, our choices, that one, the other or both are manifest. Yoda's last words to Luke were:

> Remember, a Jedi's strength flows from the Force. But beware. Anger, fear, aggression. The dark side are they. Once you start down the dark path, forever will it dominate your destiny.

These words are similar to the words Yoda spoke to the young Anakin before the Jedi Council.

MACE WINDU: Be mindful of your feelings...

KI-ADI: Your thoughts dwell on your mother.

ANAKIN: I miss her.

YODA: Afraid to lose her…I think.

ANAKIN: What's that got to do with anything?

YODA: Everything. Fear is the path to the dark side…fear leads to anger…anger leads to hate…hate leads to suffering.

The choice is ours. We are not controlled by an external power, seen or unseen. It is all within us…the power to choose…the power to act…we determine our own fate. Our life is a movie, our movie. We are the lead actor, writer, director, editor, and producer all wrapped up into one person.

How do we make the proper choices? By staying in harmony with the flow of the Tao. *Wu wei*. Practicing humility, simplicity, patience, and acceptance. By remembering your innate self, that is *P'u*. Proper choices are made by walking your path, that is the Tao.

Some say that my teaching is nonsense.
Others call it lofty but impractical.
But to those who have looked inside themselves,
This nonsense makes perfect sense.
And to those who put it into practice,
This loftiness has roots that go deep.
                                        —Chapter 67

One of the concepts that helps you in actual moment to moment living is that of focus.

> **ANAKIN:** Master Qui-Gon, sir, I do not wish to be a problem.

> **QUI-GON:** You won't be Annie…I'm not allowed to train you, so I want you to watch me and be mindful…always remember, your focus determines your reality.

A fundamental fact of consciousness is that we take on the attributes and energy of that upon which we focus are attention. That is why your focus determines your reality. When your attention is focused and unified, your capacity to function becomes heightened. Energy follows attention. Wherever you focus your attention your energy follows. Whatever you put your attention on develops and grows. Focus on the present moment.

On Dagobah, before taking Luke on as a student he spoke these words to Obi-Wan about Luke.

> This one a long time have I watched. All his life has he looked away…to the future, to the

horizon. Never his mind on where he was. Hmm? What he was doing.

Hope, that you can be better or that it can be better, takes away from the present moment, not allowing you to be where you are and who you are. Logically, the present moment is the only moment in which you can actually live. No matter how accurate your thoughts of the past or your predictions of the future, they take away from the present moment…the only moment in which you can actually live. As long as what you are doing at the moment is exactly what you are doing at that moment and nothing else, you are at one with yourself and with what you are doing and in harmony with the Tao. That is what the Buddha meant when he said, "When I eat…I eat, when I walk…I walk."

How does planning fit into present moment living? The opening scene in *The Phantom Menace* addresses this question.

OBI-WAN: I have a bad feeling about this.

QUI-GON: I don't sense anything.

OBI-WAN: It's not about the mission, Master, it's something…elsewhere…elusive…

QUI-GON: Don't center on your anxiety, Obi-Wan. Keep your concentration here and now where it belongs.

OBI-WAN: Master Yoda says I should be mindful of the future…

QUI-GON: …but not at the expense of the moment. Be

mindful of the living Force, my young Padawan.

Be mindful of the future but do not let it distract from the present. The best way to prepare for any future event is to be fully in your present moment now.

Do not overlook the plain truth of the present moment. Too often, in day to day living, you miss this exquisite moment with its powerful spiritual quality.

Let the Tao be present in your life
And you will become genuine.
Let it be present in your family
And your family will flourish.
Let it be present in your country
And your country will be an example
To all countries in the world.
Let it be present in the universe
And the universe will sing.

How do I know this is true?
By looking inside myself.

—Chapter 54

As you let the Tao be present in your life remember to be present in your own life. A measure of success is not necessarily how you fare in competition, but how fully you live your life…each moment.

CHAPTER ELEVEN

YODA AS THE SAGE MASTER

The master is the embodiment of the Tao. Yoda is the embodiment of the master.

> *The ancient masters were profound and subtle.*
> *Their wisdom was unfathomable.*
> *There is no way to describe it;*
> *All we can describe is their appearance.*
> **—Chapter 15**

Lao Tzu might as well have talking about Yoda.

They were careful
As someone crossing an iced-over stream.
Alert as a warrior in enemy territory.
Courteous as a guest.
Fluid as melting ice.
Shapeable as a block of wood.
Receptive as a valley.
Clear as a glass of water.

—Chapter 15

Allow me to describe the traits of a master, as paraphrased from the *Tao Te Ching* as interpreted by Stephen Mitchell.

TRAITS OF A MASTER

Acts without doing anything
Acts but does not expect
Teaches without saying anything
Does not take sides
Has but does not possess
Does not talk but acts
Accepts himself
Makes use of solitude
Leads by emptying mind of concepts, judgements and desires, filling them with a sense of their original identity
Observes the world but trusts his own inner vision
Does not seek fulfillment, not seeking, not expecting, she is present and can welcome all things
Travels all day without leaving home (without losing touch with who she really is)
Is available to all people and does not reject anyone
Is ready to use all situations and does not waste anything
Sees things as they are, without trying to control them, letting them go and residing at the center of the circle
Does his job and then stops, he understands that the universe is forever out of control (of his own tiny personal conscious self) and that trying to dominate events goes against the Tao
Does not try to convince others because he believes in himself
Does not need others' approval because he is content with himself
Does not try to be powerful thus he is truly powerful
Does nothing yet he leaves nothing undone (no expectations, no regrets no residue)

Dwells in reality and lets all illusions go

Allows things to happen, she shapes events as they come and then steps out of the way

Arrives without leaving, sees the light without looking, and achieves without doing a thing

Is good to all people and trusts all people

Never expects results and thus he is never disappointed

Is never disappointed thus his spirit never grows old

Lets all things come and go effortlessly, without desire

Never reaches for the greatness thus she achieves greatness

When confronted by a difficulty, stops and gives herself to it

Takes action by letting things take their course

Remains as calm at the end as at the beginning

Acts without expectation, succeeds without taking credit, and does not think that she is better than anyone else

Remains serene in the midst of sorrow

Fulfills her own obligations and corrects her own mistakes

Does what she needs to do and demands nothing of others

Has no possessions, the more he does for others the happier he is

Lives with unconditional sincerity, eradicates duality, and celebrates the equality of things

You have now experienced my humble understanding of the Tao, expressed through the imperfect medium of words. This knowledge of the Tao will not necessarily make your life easier. You still have to wake up in the morning. You still have to keep right on being a human. You still have to go to sleep at night and wake up in the morning and start all over again. However, if you choose to walk the path you will have the tools to live each moment to the fullest and what more is there than that.

The Tao is a path…the only logical act is to travel it.

HAVE A WONDERFUL TRIP!

BIBLIOGRAPHY

1. Mitchell, Stephen, translator. *Tao Te Ching*. New York: HarperCollins Publishers, 1988.

2. Bouzereau, Laurent. *STAR WARS The Annotated Screenplays*. New York: Ballantine Books, 1977.

3. Lucas, George. *STAR WARS Episode I The Phantom Menace Illustrated Screenplay*. New York: Ballantine Publishing Group, 1999.

4. Ming-Dao, Deng. *Everyday Tao*. San Francisco: HarperSanFrancisco, 1996.

5. Freke, Timothy. *Taoist Wisdom Daily Teachings from the Taoist Sages*. New York: Sterling Publishing Company, Inc., 1999.

6. Wei, Henry. *The Guiding Light of Lao Tzu*. Wheaton, Illinois: The Theosophical Publishing House, 1982.

7. Palmer, Wendy. *The Intuitive Body Aikido as a Clairsentient Practice*. Berkeley, Ca.: North Atlantic Books, 1994.

8. Hoff, Benjamin. *The Tao of Pooh*. Toronto, Ontario: Penguin Books, 1982.

ABOUT THE AUTHOR

John M. Porter, M.D. has been studying the Tao and traveling along the Way for the past ten years. He integrates his practice of Taoism with the practice of Aikido. He is a Professor of Clinical Surgery and the Chief Trauma Surgeon at the University of Arizona. He lives with his wife, Lee, and two children, Jayson and Jourdan, in Tucson, Arizona.

Printed in the United States
210383BV00003B/355/A